A NEW BELIEVERS **GUIDE** TO CHRISTIANITY

A NEW BELIEVERS **GUIDE** TO CHRISTIANITY
........*What Now!?*

JOHN D. BURRIS

XULON PRESS

Xulon Press
2301 Lucien Way #415
Maitland, FL 32751
407.339.4217
www.xulonpress.com

© 2018 by John D. Burris

All rights reserved solely by the author. The author guarantees all contents are original and do not infringe upon the legal rights of any other person or work. No part of this book may be reproduced in any form without the permission of the author. The views expressed in this book are not necessarily those of the publisher.

Unless otherwise indicated, Scripture quotations taken from the English Standard Version (ESV). Copyright © 2001 by Crossway, a publishing ministry of Good News Publishers. Used by permission. All rights reserved.

Scripture quotations taken from the Holy Bible, New International Version (NIV). Copyright © 1973, 1978, 1984, 2011 by Biblica, Inc.™. Used by permission. All rights reserved.

Scripture quotations taken from the New King James Version (NKJV). Copyright © 1982 by Thomas Nelson, Inc. Used by permission. All rights reserved.

Printed in the United States of America.

ISBN-13: 9781545630198

ACKNOWLEDGEMENTS

To my children: Braiden, Ivy and Keira.
To my wife Jodie, and my mother Cindy.
To all believers everywhere, believers
who no longer feel the presence of God
(or maybe never have),
and to anyone truly seeking;
May this book excite and inspire you
to pursue a personal relationship
with Jesus Christ…. the Creator of
the heavens and the earth!

TABLE OF CONTENTS

Foreword ix
Introduction xi

Chapter 1 Get Baptized 1
Chapter 2 Join a Healthy, Well-
           Balanced Church 5
Chapter 3 Communicate with God 11
Chapter 4 The Deity of Jesus 19
Chapter 5 The Trinity 21
Chapter 6 The Resurrection 27
Chapter 7 Creation 31
Chapter 8 The Eternal State 39

Conclusion 47

FOREWORD

So you gave your life to Jesus Christ! Congratulations! You have just taken the most important step that you will ever take in your entire life. Nothing else you ever personally do for the rest of your life is more important than what you have already done! You have made the most important decision that you will ever make in your entire life! Most importantly, you made the RIGHT decision.

So now, let's take a look at the good news. You have ALREADY made the MOST IMPORTANT decision of your entire life! Now you might ask: "So what's the bad news?"

Okay, I'll tell you. The bad news is...well...there really isn't any bad news! You have ALREADY and

CORRECTLY made the most important decision of your entire life!

I think you are starting to get the picture. You are now a brother- or sister-in-Christ. YOU ARE in the kingdom of God! But perhaps you do have one question. If it is the one I think you have, it's the reason why you are reading this book right now. That question is, "Ya, I gave my life to Christ… NOW WHAT!?

What a great question! This book is a guide to help you find some answers to this important question of "What now?" This short book will give you an outline and provide one possible path that you may take to start your journey with God.

INTRODUCTION

You have accepted Jesus Christ. You have basically said, " I am A sinner. I know You are God, and I want to serve and follow You for eternity!" What an awesome decision! But now you are asking yourself, "What now? What do I do next?"

First things first. Get baptized! In the next chapter, we will look into what baptism symbolizes. But for now, simply know that baptism should be the first act of obedience after you say "Yes" to Jesus Christ. You have told yourself and God that you want to follow Him. So, through baptism, you can publicly declare your faith.

Assuming you just ran out and got baptized or if you are more of the type who says to yourself, "I think I'll read a little more before I put any of what this book says into action," it's now time to stop and talk about how this book is laid out.

Imagine if you will that a Sunday church service has just ended. You and a friend (who is a believer and can answer questions you have about Christianity) have decided to go to your local coffee house and talk about what this whole Christianity thing is. Well, in that same situation is how you should envision yourself as you read through this book. It's simply you and a Christian friend in a relaxed, laid-back, no-pressure atmosphere—just one friend helping another friend start to discover his new journey with God.

That being said, the most important thing for you to know about this book is that it is simply A GUIDE! It is not intended to be something you have to follow step by step. Your journey with God is unique to you. Just as no two human relationships are exactly the same, your relationship with your heavenly Father will not be exactly the same as anyone else's. It will be unique between you and God.

As a new believer, it may be hard to figure out what to do next once you have begun your relationship with God. Don't worry! This book is designed to be your guide. It will lay out ONE POSSIBLE PATH for you to follow over the first few weeks or months of the journey you are beginning with Jesus Christ. You can follow that path however you choose. While following it step by step will be very beneficial, your journey with God is yours. So feel free to apply different chapters to your journey as you see fit.

Also, now that you have begun a relationship with Jesus Christ, you may hear Christians using words that you don't understand yet. Let's just call it "Christian lingo." This book will try to remove as much of the Christian lingo as possible. You can then feel like you are listening to a friend explaining concepts that might be new to you. Otherwise, it would mean stopping to explain every time a Christian-lingo word comes up in the conversation. But rest assured, as your journey with Jesus Christ continues and your relationship with Him grows,

Christian lingo will become as familiar to you as your native language!

So back to that original question: "What now? I gave my life to Jesus Christ, but what now? What do I do next?" The following is an outline to help you start on your journey. Now don't worry, you won't be left hanging with only an outline. Each subject in this outline will be addressed in a chapter of this book.

1) Get baptized.
2) Join a healthy, well-balanced church.
3) Communicate with God. (Pray and read the Bible.)
4) The Deity of Jesus (Know Jesus is God.)
5) The Trinity (Apprehend the Trinity.)
6) Resurrection (Realize why the resurrection is so special.)
7) Creation (Understand where you came from.)
8) The eternal state (Discover where you are going.)

Once you have a basic grasp of these eight topics, you will have a solid foundation for your faith and be well on your way to developing a wonderful relationship with Jesus Christ.

One final concept needs to be covered before you start flipping through the pages of this book. As you read this book, always be aware that the information you are receiving is only a brief overview—a starting point, if you will. It is up to you to dig deep into each topic to fully grasp its significance and relevance to your life. Finally, it is important to realize that while reading books written by men can be helpful and beneficial, reading THE BOOK (the Bible) authored by God Himself will always be the greatest inspiration, authority and help that you will ever find in written form!

CHAPTER 1

Get Baptized

What is baptism? By definition, *baptism* is "a symbolic act that is done after a person gives his life to Jesus Christ." Being baptized should be the first act of obedience that is done as a new Christian. During baptism, a believer in Jesus Christ is asked to express his faith. Next, he is submerged in water and brought back up out of the water.

This three-step action represents one complete symbolic act. So let's break it down and take a look at what each step symbolizes. First, you confess your belief in God. You are then submerged in water to represent the death of your old self. As you are brought back up out of the water, it represents your being born as a new creation in Jesus

Christ. Baptism is symbolic of your joining Jesus in His death, burial and resurrection.

The symbolic act of baptism is a mirror of a spiritual transformation, which takes place when you put your faith in God. When you confess your sins, ask Jesus to forgive those sins and declare that you want to follow Jesus and become part of His kingdom, an *internal transformation* happens. The Holy Spirit enters and dwells within you. Your body now becomes the "temple" for the Holy Spirit. So *baptism* is "the outward expression of your internal transformation." You are stating to the world that you have been transformed by the power of God. Baptism is a declaration that you now choose to follow Him!

Baptism is often likened to being married. Wearing a wedding ring declares to the world that you belong to someone. Not wearing one doesn't mean you are not married, but no one knows for sure that you belong to someone. Just like a wedding ring shows that you are married, baptism shows that you belong to Jesus.

Now if you are not married, take a second to remember back to the time when you fell in love with someone. You knew it and felt it deep down in your soul. So, naturally, you told that special someone how you felt. Then you wanted your friends, family and the whole world to know!

Well, in a nutshell, that example is what baptism is. When you get baptized, you are confirming to yourself and telling the world (through the symbolic act of baptism) that you love Jesus, need Jesus and will follow Him forever.

CHAPTER 2

Join a Healthy, Well-balanced Church

To join a healthy, well-balanced church, an individual must first find one! What does it mean to find, and how do you know when you have found a healthy, well-balanced church? Well, churches, like people, come in many shapes, sizes and flavors. It's important to realize that no church is perfect! Each one has its own strengths and weaknesses. However, there are both healthy churches and unhealthy churches. The degree of healthiness or unhealthiness will vary from church to church, but there are some key foundations for which to look in a healthy church.

The main aspects of a healthy, well-balanced church are a pastor who leads and a church family who participates in prayer, praise and the proclamation of God's Word. Now *prayer, praise* and *proclamation* are probably three unfamiliar, fancy words, but gaining an understanding of them is really quite simple. Let's break them down individually.

1) Prayer. *Prayer* is simply "talking with God." When you are looking for prayer in a church service, you should notice one main constant. The leaders of the service—the worship leader, the news and update guys, the senior or lead pastor—should all (or at the very least, one of them) throughout the service, pray to God.

2) Praise. *Praise* simply means "worship; to lift up or elevate God." In many cases, praise is singing songs to the Lord. It is also when God is given praise during prayer. During your Christian journey, you will notice that, as you start to praise God, you will find a beautiful truth. As you praise, you sense the presence of the Lord.

3) Proclamation of the Word. *Proclaiming* means "speaking and teaching ABOUT GOD, who God is and His nature." Everything He has revealed to us comes through the Bible, the primary way God communicates to us. And therefore, reading from and learning from the Bible should be the main way God's Word is taught when attending church.

One helpful way to discover what church should be is to take a look at what church should not be. Church is not so much about what God can do for us all of the time. Church is not about how we can figure out some formula to try to get God to do what WE WANT. If you walk out of church every Sunday and feel like you sat through a "self-help" or a "feel-good" seminar, or you are learning a formula or a way to get God to do what YOU want, well, those feelings are red flags! On most occasions, you should walk out of church having learned principles and life lessons about God the Father, Jesus, or the Holy Spirit. In time, you will learn to tell when the Holy Spirit is speaking through your pastors and worship leaders; and believe me, when that happens, the message is overwhelmingly about what YOU can do for the Lord, not what the Lord can do for YOU.

All that being explained, your next question might be: "So how do I go about discovering if a church I might want to attend is participating in prayer, praise and the proclamation of the Word?" The first and easiest step is to read the church's core beliefs. These stated beliefs will give you an understanding of what the church believes, what ideas are most important to the church and the direction that the church is headed.

Most churches will have a written core set of beliefs or something similar. Most likely, what a church believes will be available on the church's website or in a printed format at the church. When you are visiting, simply ask someone at the church, and that person will gladly steer you in the right direction. Keep in mind, when you are looking over a church's core beliefs, you should get a sense that prayer, praise and the proclamation of the Word are important and are at the forefront of that church's program.

As already stated, these suggestions are simply a brief summary of how to find a healthy, well-balanced church. A plethora of helpful materials are available to give you a more knowledgeable grasp as to what church God is calling you to join.

WHY SHOULD I GO TO CHURCH?

Now that you know WHAT to look for in a church, perhaps you are wondering WHY you should attend church. First, it's important to understand that there are no "Lone-Ranger" Christians; that is to say, no believer should go through life with the idea that it's "just God and me." The reason for this? God is relational! Just as you and God have a relationship, God has designed your local church to be a relational community for you and other believers. For this reason, the church is called the "body of Christ." The church is designed to give you guidance, comfort, friendship, instruction and help you mature in your relationship with God.

Our ultimate authority is Jesus Christ; however, God has set up the church to be His "body of believers" here on earth. While it is true, the people who lead those churches are flawed and sinful—just like the rest of us; it is important to remember that Jesus Christ is the head of the church! Therefore, it is essential for each one of us to be in a healthy, well-balanced church for our spiritual growth and maturity. A important truth that you will discover on your Christian journey is that not only do you need the "body of Christ" (the church) but the "body of Christ" (the church) NEEDS YOU!

CHAPTER 3

Communicate with God

Pray and read the Bible.

The next step on your journey with God is learning how to communicate with Him. The primary way to have an effective two-way communication is through reading the Bible and prayer. God communicates with us in many ways; however, the principal way He chooses to communicate with us is through His Word, which is the Bible. Another way God communicates with us is through prayer, which is also the primary way that WE communicate with Him.

Your relationship with Jesus is exactly that—a relationship. In a relationship here on earth, we learn about each other, talk to each other and spend time with each other. We must take these same steps in order to build our relationship with God. The main way we learn about God, and a large part of how He communicates with us, is through reading the Bible.

God is the Author of the Bible. He inspired the writing of the Bible so He could communicate to you about Himself! Imagine for a second that your dad had written a very LONG book to specifically tell you all about himself. Then your dad gave you this book to read and explore. Wouldn't that book be an amazing gift! This is the very reason why God authored the Bible. The Bible has eloquently been referred to as God's 66 love letters written specifically for you! However, in contrast to reading the book from your earthly father, it is important to realize that when you read the Bible, you are interacting with the mind of God! Stop and think about that connection for a second. When you read the Bible, your human mind is interacting with the infinite (no beginning and no end) mind of God!

This statement alone should spark a lifetime of excitement in your mind as well as in your soul.

God also communicates with His children (Christian believers) in other ways, including through dreams and visions, when we pray and when we worship—to name only a few. So as you can see, God has and will make Himself known. He has and will continue to communicate with us. The only question left to answer is, "Do we want to build a relationship with Him?"

Now you might be thinking to yourself: *that God can communicate with us is awesome, but how are we, finite (having limits or bounds) human beings supposed to be able to communicate with an infinite (limitless or endless) God?* That's a great question! And the answer to that question is prayer! Prayer is quite simply our talking with God; and if we will listen, God's talking to us.

Unfortunately, many people think that when we pray to God, prayer is only our asking God for things or our simply bringing our problems or our requests to Him. While asking for our needs is definitely

PART of prayer, it's only a very small part. When we are communicating with God through prayer, we should be building a relationship. Think about it like this: you have a friend here on earth, and every time you meet, all you do is tell that friend about your problems, wanting him to quickly fix them for you. How much do you think your friendship would grow? The truth is, it wouldn't. In actuality, that relationship wouldn't be a friendship at all! Instead, that relationship would be more akin to asking a magic genie to fix all of your problems and grant you all of your wants in life. Unfortunately, this illustration is all too often how Christians approach prayer with God.

Now, if you and that same friend spend the time conversing about your life, joy, hopes, dreams, goals, and you listened to your friend tell you the same, you would be truly building a relationship that will continually deepen and grow. Therefore, when you pray to God, a simple approach is talking and listening to God like you and your best friend are sitting in your living room, casually chatting away. Listen to what He says to you and share all of yourself with Him.

So that's the basic idea of how we communicate with God. The wonderful thing is we live in an age where many great books and resources are available to help you explore the amazing relationship you can build with God through reading the Bible and prayer.

WHERE TO START READING IN THE BIBLE

You just read this subheading, and you are likely thinking to yourself: *Well, that's obvious! It's a book; I'll start reading at the beginning.*

Guess what? That subtitle is not a trick statement. You would be right! The very beginning of the Bible is a great place to start, but it's not the ONLY place you can start!

You are probably thinking, *Wait, what? Hold on a second. That doesn't make any sense!*

As a new believer to Christianity, you may have never read a single verse in the Bible. If that's the case, you might like to know a few things, which will be a huge help to you. First, the Bible is unlike any book you have ever read! Every book you have read throughout your lifetime has been authored by men. The Bible, however, has been authored by God Himself. Therefore, not only is it a natural book, but it is also a supernatural spiritual Book! The Bible is a *natural* book in the sense that it's ink on paper, penned by men. The Bible is *supernatural* because the Spirit of God inspired those men to write down God's very words and thoughts to compile the scriptures.

Therefore, the Bible is a Book completely and solely authored by God Himself. God used 40 human authors to pen a collection of 66 books within one Book—the Bible. Because of this, you can read the Bible in a different way than you could a normal book.

Let's compare a typical novel to the Bible. In the novel, you have to read all the way through, starting at the very beginning. Most (but not all) books are constructed in a fashion where the story builds on the settings, the introduction of each character, and the chapter divisions. You have to read and understand chapter 1 to be able to understand chapter 2 and so forth. In contrast, all 66 books of the Bible point to the main theme, God. The whole Bible is about Jesus, which is why any book contained inside the Bible can be your starting point.. As Martin Luther put it, "The Bible is the cradle wherein Christ is laid." Therefore, you can just as easily start reading in the book of John as you can in the book of Genesis. Eventually, you will want to read through the entire Bible, but as far as the sequence goes, there is no right or wrong way as to how you read the individual 66 books that comprise the Bible.

Now there are many great reading plans, which you can find and research on your own to help you to find your path of reading through the Bible. The important thing is that you START reading God's Word. The more you read, the more you will understand God and the deeper you will build your relationship with Him. On a side note, if you are at a loss as to where to start reading, the Gospel of John in the New Testament is a place where many pastors suggest new believers start. There is a very good reason for this. The whole Bible is about Jesus Christ, which is why it's great to start with Him. Everything in the Old Testament points to the fact that people need rescuing. Jesus Christ is that rescuer, but it's hard to see that without first understanding who Jesus is and what He did on earth. The book of John will give you this foundation. So don't worry, wherever you choose to start reading the Bible, be assured, God has saturated Himself throughout ALL the pages of scripture!

CHAPTER 4

The Deity of Jesus

Know Jesus is God.

Did you know that Jesus is God? Yes! You do? That's great! Because plenty of people think Jesus was only a man like any other man—just some guy who walked this earth over two thousand years ago. A small group of people even claim the historical Jesus never existed. But the truth is, you would be hard-pressed to find ANY creditable scholar who would say that there WASN'T an actual historical man named Jesus who walked this earth some two thousand years ago! Furthermore, by studying numerous secular (non-Christian) and Christian historians, you can quickly and easily confirm the historical accuracy of the biblical man named Jesus.

A well-established FACT is that the man named Jesus (as recorded in the Bible) lived and walked this earth some two thousand years ago. Unfortunately, many people think Jesus was only a prophet or a great man—not God. But the mother of all questions is *who did Jesus say He was?*

The answer is this: Jesus said HE IS GOD! Jesus told the Jews He was God. Jesus told the Jewish religious leaders of His time that He was God! Jesus agreed with Thomas when Thomas worshiped Jesus by saying "my Lord and my God." Last, but not least, Jesus claimed to posses the very attributes of God!

Jesus clearly claimed to be God. And all throughout the Bible Jesus is claimed to be God. So you can rest assured that Jesus isn't simply a great man or prophet of a world religion. He is the Creator of the universe, the One who spoke and the universe leaped into existence. He is the infinite One who created all people and holds all things together. He is God!

CHAPTER 5

The Trinity

Apprehend the Trinity.

So exactly what do Christians mean when they say or use the words "the Trinity"? The simple answer is that Christians use this word *Trinity* to express what is meant when they are talking about God.

If you are scratching your head right now, be assured that it's okay. Let's take a minute to dive into what a Christian means when he uses the word *Trinity*. But before starting, here is a little disclaimer: you will NOT find the word *Trinity* in the Bible. This word is used by Christians to best describe what they mean when they are talking about God.

First, as a Christian, you are *monotheistic*—just a fancy word to say that you believe in only ONE God. God's own revelation of Himself to us (which is the Bible) is very clear that there is only one God! As a Christian, you believe in only one God! As a Christian, you believe the Father is God, Jesus Christ is God, and the Holy Spirit is God.

Wait, what? By now you may be scratching your head and thinking to yourself: *this doesn't make any sense!* Don't worry, the statement (there is only one God, and the Father is God; Jesus Christ is God; and the Holy Spirit is God) should give you pause! It very well might make you ask a logical question: "How in the world can this be?!"

Two main factors need to be grasped that will help give this statement context. To review, God is infinite, and you are finite. There are times when God is telling you something about Himself that you can still APPREHEND what He is saying even if you cannot fully COMPREHEND what He wants to communicate to you. It is also important to remember that God communicates with you in many ways.

However, the main way He has chosen to reveal Himself to you is through the Bible. God has used many humans to write and record the Bible, but never forget that God is the divine Author! He has authored the Bible so that you may know what He has chosen to reveal and share with you. That being stated, the following is what God has chosen to reveal and share (through the Bible) concerning Himself.

There are three *planks* or "points" concerning the Trinity.

1) There is only one God.
2) The Father is God, Jesus is God and the Holy Spirit is God.
3) The Father, the Son (Jesus) and the Holy Spirit are all eternally distinct.

An effective way to explain the Trinity is to say there is one WHAT and three WHOS. There is one God (what) in nature or essence and three persons (whos) of the Godhead that are eternally distinct.

Another way to put it would be to say that the Bible is articulating that there is one God with respect to His nature, but within that one God (or within the Godhead), there are personal self-distinctions.

The Bible is crystal clear that there is only one God. The Bible is also crystal clear that Jesus Christ is God. The Bible is crystal clear that the Holy Spirit is God, and the Bible is crystal clear that the Father is God. As a result of those personal self-distinctions, the Bible teaches that the Father loves the Son (Jesus), the Father sends the Son, the Son prays to the Father, the Son sends the Counselor (the Holy Spirit) and so on. The Bible furthermore makes the distinction that the Father, Jesus and the Holy Spirit are eternally distinct, which is to say the Father never becomes Jesus, Jesus never becomes the Holy Spirit, the Holy Spirit never becomes the Father etc.

Also important is to understand what the Trinity is not. The Trinity is not three different gods, each with his own natures. Worshiping, for example, Zeus, Poseidon or Aries from Greek mythology would be considered *polytheism*, the belief in multiple gods. The Trinity is also not the belief that God is only the Father. But the Father does take on different forms such as Jesus and the Holy Spirit, which would be called *modalism*.

It would be very instructive and helpful to remember that, as Christians, we may never fully comprehend every concept that God has revealed to us through His Word (the Bible). We must always keep in mind the fact that God is infinite, and we are finite beings. As a finite human mind interacting with the infinite mind of God, we may never be fully able to comprehend the idea of the Trinity. We can, however, *apprehend* what the Bible clearly teaches: there IS only one God, the Father IS God, Jesus IS God, and the Holy Spirit IS God!

CHAPTER 6

Resurrection

Realize why it is so special.

Have you ever stopped and considered the main difference between Christianity and every other religion in the world? They all had their holy men or their prophet, but only Jesus Christ made the claim He was actually God! While all of the holy men and prophets of all the other religions around the world have died and are in their graves, Jesus Christ is still alive. He proved His claim that He is God! He proved this claim through His resurrection!

Why is it of the utmost importance that Jesus Christ has been resurrected? The apostle Paul has answered this question for us. *"...if Christ has not been raised, our preaching is useless and so is your faith"* (I Corinthians 15:14, NIV). Wow! That is a huge statement! If Jesus Christ has not been raised, then your faith is useless. Yup! That is the case! The reason is simple. Jesus Christ claimed to be God. When He was asked how He could prove this claim, Jesus responded by telling them that when He was killed, He would rise again after three days (John 2:19). Therefore, either Jesus was resurrected after three days and proved He was God, or He did not rise after three days, and our faith is useless!

As you can see, the resurrection of Jesus Christ is the most important historical fact and the anchor of your Christian faith. Thankfully, there are many ways to know that Jesus Christ was resurrected from the dead. Actually, the resurrection of Jesus Christ is the greatest **FEAT** in history! First was the **F**atal torment of Jesus Christ. Next is the **E**mpty tomb. Then came the post-resurrection **A**ppearances of Jesus Christ to His disciples and many other people. Finally, there is the **T**ransformation of His disciples from scared sheep to lions of the faith. This transformation happened because they saw and experienced the resurrected Christ!

Because of these facts and many more, you can rest assured that Jesus Christ DID RISE FROM THE GRAVE! Your faith is firmly anchored in the fact that, because He rose from the grave, Jesus Christ proved He is God!

As always, this book has laid out a path for you to investigate these topics on your own. The point is to INVESTIGATE! Your faith is rooted in history, evidence and fact; therefore, you should not be afraid to seek answers!

CHAPTER 7

Creation

Understand where you came from.

What is the meaning of life? Mankind has been attempting to answer this question for their entire existence. Almost certainly, this question has crossed your mind at some point in your life. Ironically, the answer to this question is quite simple; but to find it, you must first take a step back. To answer that question concerning the meaning of life, a person must first address the matter of creation. How was everything created? How did we get here? How did this planet, our galaxy and even the entire universe come into existence?

Philosophical naturalism (the worldview that supports evolution) has narrowed down the answer to the origin of the universe to three explanations:

1) The universe is simply an illusion.
2) The universe originated from nothing.
3) The universe has eternally existed.

While you are encouraged to examine these theories on your own, you can rest assured they have all been disproven by science. By science? Yep! You read that statement correctly! Christians use science! As a matter of fact, science doesn't tell us anything; scientists do! Science is simply the process people use to support a theory. A scientist or a person using science is required to follow the truth wherever it may lead.

All scientific data needs to be gathered, and all data needs to be interpreted. Who does that? Scientists do; the data doesn't gather itself, and the data doesn't interpret itself. Unfortunately, most non-Christians approach science with the preconceived idea that nothing is supernatural (outside of nature or the material universe). Therefore, they exclude any supernatural evidence even if that is where the scientific evidence points!

As Christians, we are open to the natural as well as the supernatural explanations. The result? Christians are free to seek truth wherever the scientific answers lead! Furthermore, the ability to know and use science only exists because of God! We wouldn't even have science if God didn't exist. A popular, modern-day myth is to believe that science and faith are somehow in opposition to each other. But the fact is, science cannot even be done unless scientists use principles and laws set forth by God! You might say evolutionists and atheists are "stealing from God" to argue against Him!

Now, you can have fun diving into the particulars of the three aforementioned possibilities regarding the creation of the universe, but allow me to sum up everything. In a scientific age, the idea that the universe is simply an illusion carries little scientific weight, while the scientific laws of cause and effect, energy conservation and entropy destroy the ideas that the universe originated from nothing or eternally existed!

If none of these evolutionary or naturalistic ideas can explain where the universe came from, then what can? Well, when you look at the universe, the solar system and the earth, you can clearly and obviously see a design. When you see a design, you inevitably know a designer is involved! Let's use a watch as an example. When looking at a watch, you clearly know that instrument of precision was designed and created by an intelligent mind. You automatically realize the watch simply didn't come into existence through chance and time. All of the pieces did not "just happen" to fit together and work. A watch clearly has a design and if the watch has a design, then it had a designer! This explanation is known as *intelligent design* (I.D., for short).

In its simplest form, I.D. states that because we see and experience and can prove design in our universe, an intelligent mind must have designed it. We call that mind God. While I.D. simply states there is a designer (and doesn't necessarily point to the God of the Bible), a mountain of provable evidence exists that Jesus Christ is the Designer and the Creator of our universe to which intelligent design points.

Now back to the question that sparked this search to find answers about creation. What is the meaning of life? Well, in creation, you have found the answer. On the one hand, if you were created out of nothing by nothing, if time and chance caused everything to form into what it is today, if blind chance has brought you into existence, if you are simply a moist robot or only molecules in motion, then the answer is...there is NO meaning to life! How could there be? As a famous modern "science guy" stated:

> I'm insignificant...I am just another speck of sand. And the earth really in the cosmic scheme of things is another speck. And the sun an unremarkable star. ...And the galaxy is a speck. I'm a speck on a speck orbiting

a speck among other specks among still other specks in the middle of specklessness. I suck.

On the other hand, however, if the answer is found in intelligent design and that designer is Jesus Christ, you are not insignificant and a completely different answer exists. God says, *"The heavens declare the glory of God; the skies proclaim the work of His hands"* (Psalm 19:1, NIV).

God is REAL! He created this planet, this galaxy, this universe and HE CREATED YOU! God, communicating through the Bible, has told you how important you are to Him! Therefore, you have meaning, a purpose and a path. There IS an answer to the question of the meaning of life, and that answer is:

TO GLORIFY GOD AND ENJOY HIM FULLY FOREVER!

The meaning of life is to GLORIFY GOD! In other words, to make Him known! And to ENJOY HIM

FULLY FOREVER by building a relationship with Him from this day through eternity! Furthermore, because there is a meaning to life, there is also a purpose. The purpose of life is to know God and to make Him known! At some point, there is a good chance you will hear a Christian complaining: "I don't know what God's "will" for my life is."

What they are really asking or what they are searching for is: "What is God's purpose or "will" for my life?" The beautiful secret is God's purpose or "will" for all Christians is the same: to know God and make Him known! As a Christian, there is no reason to worry or stress about finding God's specific purpose for your life. As you follow your general purpose (to know God and to make Him known), God will direct you to a specific path and purpose He has set forth just for you! In God's infinite wisdom, He has done all the work for you. Instead of YOUR trying to figure out your purpose, all that is required is for you to follow the general purpose God has set out for everyone. Then He (not you) will fine tune your specific path; and throughout the whole process (no matter how long it takes), you will still be serving His purpose or "will" for your life!

So as you can clearly see, how you view your origin will surely determine how you live your life. Sadly, millions of people are still looking for the answer to the meaning of life—not ever considering the possibility of looking for the answer in the question of creation.

CHAPTER 8

The Eternal State

Discover where you are going.

Have you ever wondered what will happen to you after you die? You might want to ponder this question for a while. As a matter of fact, knowing what is going to happen to you after you die might just change the way you see things. And, in turn, it may even change the way you live your life!

Many Christians believe that when you die, you simply go to heaven. But what exactly does that phrase "go to heaven" mean?

If an unbeliever asked for further clarification, most Christians would explain by saying: "Your spirit goes to heaven" or "Your spirit is in heaven with

God." When pressed on what that answer actually means, many Christians who hold this view simply don't have an answer. They might say, "I haven't actually given it much thought," or "It simply means we are in heaven with God."

Uh, okay, but that unbeliever has only been given a very vague answer. If I were an unbeliever, I would still be scratching my head, wondering what happens to a Christian once he dies. In the best-case scenario, those Christians really haven't given it much thought. In the worst-case scenario, those answers sometimes seem as if a Christian is saying, "I'm not sure what happens when I die, but I'm covered—no matter what happens." In some cases, it feels like just in case they die, they have bought themselves a spiritual insurance policy. And that spiritual "fire" insurance policy will keep them out of a bad place and get them into a good place—whatever or wherever that good place is.

Uhhhhhh...hello? We are all going to die of our last accident or disease (unless we are alive when Jesus Christ comes back). The death rate is 1 for

1. We are all going to make it, and if that's the case, shouldn't you want to know what is waiting for you next?

While it is technically true that when we die we will go to heaven, our eternal state encompasses so much more! Not only that, the fact that we will exist for about 70 years (on average) in this life and exist for eternity in the life to come should at least make us want to know as much as possible about our eternal state.

Now that we understand why we should want to know about the eternal state, let's walk through what God has revealed to us about what happens to a Christian after he dies. As a Christian, you need to realize that you will live FOREVER in the presence of God. So let's take a look at what an eternal existence with God looks like! First, you live your life here on earth with the Lord! This is true because His Spirit now dwells within you. Second, after you die, your spirit goes to be with the Lord. Last, your body is resurrected, and your spirit is reunited with your resurrected body. So, there are three stages of your existence:

1) Life
2) Life after life
3) Life after life after life

Now I know these three stages are a mouthful, but stop and chew on them for a minute. I promise they will make sense.

Let's start with *life*. A fact many Christians tend to overlook is that our eternal existence with God does not start after we die. It starts the moment you accept Jesus Christ! You get to start your eternal existence with God right then! The first leg of your eternal existence is happening right now! God's Spirit lives inside of you, and you get to communicate and build your relationship with Jesus Christ in the here and now—not just after you die.

Next comes *life after life*. That's right. There is a life after this one! God has made this fact very clear. When you die, your body "goes to the ground," and your spirit is with the Lord. As the apostle Paul put it in 2 Corinthians 5:8, *"...absent from the body and to be present with the Lord."* So what does that verse mean?

Well, the first mistake that many modern-day Christians make is they are thinking of heaven as a place—a location, if you will. But heaven (at this time) isn't a physical place (location); rather, it is a relational reality. When you are absent from the body and present with the Lord, you are not a physical being. Therefore, you can't be in a physical place. So heaven at this point isn't physical; it's relational! When your body dies, you will be in conscious, personal, relational contact with the Lord. Just as you have built a relationship with God here on earth, your spirit will continue to consciously enjoy that relationship in the presence of the Lord!

Finally comes *life after life after life*. This is the glorious final state that we will enjoy for all eternity. While we don't know the exact point in time that this will happen, we do know it will happen when Jesus Christ comes back a second time. When

Jesus Christ appears a second time, the nonphysical aspect of our humanity is joined with the physical aspect of our humanity. Our physical body is resurrected immortal, imperishable, incorruptible. While every atom may not be the same, there will be continuity between the body we have now and our glorified body. We will be able to recognize each other in our glorified bodies. Your resurrected body will be both spiritual and physical, similar to Jesus' resurrected body. To be clear, your resurrected body will not be a new or a second body. It will be YOUR body, perfected through the power of God! In short, you will be the perfect you!

The story of the Bible from beginning to end is one of redemption. You have paradise lost in Genesis, paradise restored in Revelation. Everything in-between is the story of redemption. The resurrection of our body is the physical redemption from a cursed, sinful body into a perfected, glorified body. And just as God will resurrect our bodies, He will also resurrect and redeem the heavens and the earth.

By turning the pages of the Bible, you can see how God has summed this all up in Revelation 21, which says:

> *Now I saw a new heaven and a new earth, for the first heaven and the first earth had passed away....³"Behold, the tabernacle of God is with men, and He will dwell with them, and they shall be His people. God Himself will be with them and be their God. ⁴And God will wipe away every tear from their eyes; there shall be no more death, nor sorrow, nor crying. There shall be no more pain, for the former things have passed away"*(vv. 1, 3-4).

CONCLUSION

Well, you made it through the book! Hopefully, you now have a solid outline of how to start your journey with God. Hopefully, you feel like you have finished that coffee-house conversation with your friend, and you now have a basic idea of who God is and how to get to know Him. If, on the other hand, this book has left you with more questions than answers, well, that's okay too!

Remember, this book is not designed to GIVE you all of the answers you are seeking. Rather, it has been designed to give you a framework and a context to know even WHAT questions to ask. It is designed to give you a basic map for you to follow over the first few weeks or months of your walk with God. It's up to you to put in the work and delve deeper into understanding these topics and any new questions they might have raised.

You have likely heard the old adage: relationships take work. Well, your relationship with your Heavenly Father is no different. While He will always do a perfect work in you, now is the time for you to roll up your sleeves and put in the effort on your side to get to know the Creator of the heavens and earth! Remember, if you have questions, all you have to do is seek out the answers. Our faith is rooted in evidence, history and truth; the answers are out there!

As a Christian, you will spend from now throughout eternity walking with God. It's important to stop and clarify that when you hear Christians using the term "your walk," it is simply Christian lingo used to encompass your journey or relationship with God. That being established, you will find your walk with God is very fluid, not a strict step-by-step process that you will have to follow to the tee. It's not a journey where, if you miss a step or get something wrong, you will have to start over from the beginning. Your journey (your walk with God) will be a fluid relationship because God is relational. It is a relationship between you and your Creator. Just like your relationships with your loved ones here on earth, your relationship with God will be fluid and ever-growing!

So go and start your journey with the Lord! Most importantly, build your relationship with Him. Spend time with Him, learn about Him, rest in Him, find peace in Him and seek to deepen your love for Him every day! But most of all, enjoy your relationship with Him, for the great news is, you already know where your journey will end:

> *Then I saw a new heaven and a new earth, for the first heaven and the first earth had passed away, and the sea was no more. ²And I saw the holy city, new Jerusalem, coming down out of heaven from God, prepared as a bride adorned for her husband. ³And I heard a loud voice from the throne*

saying, "Behold, the dwelling place of God is with man. He will dwell with them, and they will be his people, and God himself will be with them as their God. ⁴He will wipe away every tear from their eyes, and death shall be no more, neither shall there be mourning, nor crying, nor pain anymore, for the former things have passed away." ⁵Then He who sat on the throne said, "Behold, I make all things new…" (Revelation 21:1-5, ESV).

ACKNOWLEDGEMENTS

First and foremost I would like to thank my Lord and savior Jesus Christ! When You said, "Seek My face," My heart said to You, "Your face, Lord, I will seek."

Secondly, I would like to acknowledge two amazing pastors, Hank Hanegraaff and Frank Turek, whose teachings have greatly influenced my beliefs and shaped my faith. Both of these amazing teachers are authors and have developed podcasts as well as radio shows. Many of the concepts about which I have written have been shape by listening to them speak, or by reading their numerous books and written material. Thank you, Hank, for your careful wisdom and insight. I most appreciate your continual call to not take what you say as truth, but to test your teachings in light of scripture. Thank you, Frank Turek , for your teaching on apologetics, specifically relating to atheist arguments and using the creation of the universe as a powerful tool in the apologetics tool box. Without both of your teachings, I doubt I would have had the courage to answer the Lord's call to write this book.

CPSIA information can be obtained
at www.ICGtesting.com
Printed in the USA
FSHW011308151118
53822FS